A Macmillan Poetry Picture Book

# Cock a DOODLE DOO!

FARMYARD Poems

Illustrations by Anna Currey

MACMILLAN CHILDREN'S BOOKS

# Acknowledgements

*The publishers wish to thank the following for permission to use copyright material:*

**Ann Bonner**, 'Mud', included in *Twinkle, Twinkle, Chocolate Bar*, John Foster, ed., Oxford University Press, 1991, by permission of the author; **Myra Cohn Livingston**, 'Lamplighter Barn' from *Wide Awake and Other Poems*. Copyright © 1959, 1987 Myra Cohn Livingston, by permission of Marian Reiner on behalf of the Estate of the author; **W. H. Davies**, 'White Sheep' from *Collected Poems*, Jonathan Cape, by permission of Dee & Griffin, trustees of the Estate of the author; **Carmen Bernos de Gasztold**, 'The Prayer of the Little Ducks' from *Prayers from the Ark*, trans. Rumer Godden, 1963, by permission of Macmillan Children's Books; **Robert Frost**, 'The Pasture' from *The Poetry of Robert Frost*, ed. Edward Connery Lathem, Jonathan Cape, by permission of Random House UK; **Ted Hughes**, 'Cow' from *The Cat and the Cuckoo*, by permission of Faber & Faber Ltd; **Grace Nichols**, 'Early Country Village Morning' from *Come On Into My Tropical Garden*, Copyright © Grace Nichols 1988, by permission of Curtis Brown Ltd on behalf of the author; **James Reeves**, 'Slowly' from *The Complete Poems for Children*, Heinemann, by permission of Laura Cecil Literary Agency on behalf of the Estate of the author; **Dr Seuss**, extract from 'Quack, Quack' from *Oh Say Can You Say*. Copyright © Dr Seuss Enterprises, L P, 1979, by permission of International Creative Management, Inc of behalf of Dr Seuss Enterprises, L P and Random House, Inc.

*Every effort has been made to trace the copyright holders but if any have been inadvertently overlooked the publishers will be pleased to make the necessary arrangement at the first opportunity.*

First published in 2000 by Macmillan Children's Books
A division of Macmillan Publishers Limited
25 Eccleston Place, London SW1W 9NF
Basingstoke and Oxford
Associated companies throughout the world.
www.panmacmillan.com

ISBN 0 333 78587 8

# Contents

# If I had a Donkey

If I had a donkey
That wouldn't go
D'you think I'd wallop him?
No! No! No!
I'd put him in a stable
And keep him nice and warm,
The best little donkey
That ever was born.
Gee up, Neddy,
Gee up, Neddy,
The best little donkey
That ever was born.

*Anon.*

# Lavender's Blue

Lavender's blue, diddle, diddle,
 Lavender's green,
When I am king, diddle, diddle,
 You shall be queen.

Call up your men, diddle, diddle,
 Set them to work,
Some to the plough, diddle, diddle,
 Some to the cart.

Some to make hay, diddle, diddle,
 Some to thresh corn,
Whilst you and I, diddle, diddle,
 Keep ourselves warm.

*Anon.*

## Jack and Jill

Jack and Jill went up the hill,
   To fetch a pail of water;
Jack fell down, and broke his crown,
   And Jill came tumbling after.

*Anon.*

# The Pasture

I'm going out to clean the pasture spring;
I'll only stop to rake the leaves away
(And wait to watch the water clear, I may):
I sha'n't be gone long.—You come too.

I'm going out to fetch the little calf
That's standing by the mother. It's so young
It totters when she licks it with her tongue.
I sha'n't be gone long.—You come too.

*Robert Frost*

# White Sheep

White sheep, white sheep
  On a blue hill,
When the wind stops
  You all stand still.
You all run away
  When the winds blow;
White sheep, white sheep,
  Where do you go?

*W. H. Davies*

# Pick, Crow, Pick

Pick, crow, pick, and have no fear,
I sit here and I don't care.
If my master chance to come,
You must fly and I must run.

*Anon.*

# Six Little Ducks

Six little ducks that I once knew,
Fat ones, skinny ones, they were too;
But the one little duck with
   the feathers on his back,
He ruled the others with his
   "Quack, quack, quack!
   Quack, quack, quack!"
He ruled the others with his
   "Quack, quack, quack!"

Down to the river they would go,
Wibble, wobble, wibble, wobble, to and fro;
But the one little duck with
   the feathers on his back,
He ruled the others with his
   "Quack, quack, quack!
   Quack, quack, quack!"
He ruled the others with his
   "Quack, quack, quack!"

Home from the river they would come,
Wibble, wobble, wibble, wobble,
  ho-hum-hum;
But the one little duck with
  the feathers on his back,
He ruled the others with his
  "Quack, quack, quack!
  Quack, quack, quack!"
He ruled the others with his
  "Quack, quack, quack!"

*Anon.*

# Little Boy Blue

Little Boy Blue come blow your horn,
The sheep's in the meadow,
   the cow's in the corn.
Where is the boy that looks after the sheep?
He's under a haycock fast asleep.
Will you wake him? No, not I!
For if I do, he's sure to cry.

*Anon.*

# Dormouse

"Now Winter is coming,"
The dormouse said,
"I must be thinking
Of going to bed."
So he curled himself up
As small as he could,
And went fast asleep
As a dormouse should.

*Lilian McCrea*

# In the Fields

One day I saw a big brown cow
Raise her head and chew,
I said, "Good morning, Mrs Cow,"
But all she said was, "Moo!"

One day I saw a woolly lamb,
I followed it quite far,
I said, "Good morning, little lamb,"
But all it said was, "Baa!"

One day I saw a dappled horse
Cropping in the hay,
I said, "Good morning, Mr Horse,"
But all he said was, "Neigh!"

*Anon.*

# Cow

The Cow comes home swinging
Her udder and singing:

"The dirt O the dirt
It does me no hurt.

And a good splash of muck
Is a blessing of luck.

O I splosh through the mud
But the breath of my cud

Is sweeter than silk.
O I splush through manure

But my heart stays pure
As a pitcher of milk."

*Ted Hughes*

# The Cock Crows in the Morn

The cock crows in the morn
To tell us to rise,
And he that lies late
Will never be wise:
For early to bed,
And early to rise,
Is the way to be healthy
And wealthy and wise.

*Anon.*

# Early Country Village Morning

Cocks crowing
Hens knowing
later they will cluck
their laying song

Houses stirring
a donkey clip-clopping
the first market bus
comes jugging along

Soon the sun will give a big yawn
and open her eye
pushing the last bit of darkness
out of the sky

*Grace Nichols*

# A Little Talk

The big brown hen and Mrs Duck
Went walking out together;
They talked about all sorts of things—
The farmyard, and the weather.
But all I heard was: "Cluck! Cluck! Cluck!"
And "Quack! Quack! Quack!" from Mrs Duck.

*Anon.*

## Quack, Quack!

We have two ducks.
　　One blue. One black.
And when our blue duck
　　goes "Quack-quack"
our black duck quickly
　　quack-quacks back.
The quacks Blue quacks
　　make her quite a quacker
but Black is a quicker
　　quacker-backer.

*Dr Seuss*

# Cock a Doodle Doo!

Cock a doodle doo!
My dame has lost her shoe;
My master's lost his fiddling stick,
And knows not what to do.

Cock a doodle doo!
What is my dame to do?
Till master finds his fiddling stick,
She'll dance without her shoe.

Cock a doodle doo!
My dame has found her shoe,
And master's found his fiddling stick,
Sing doodle doodle doo!

Cock a doodle doo!
My dame will dance with you,
While master fiddles his fiddling stick,
For dame and doodle doo.

*Anon.*

# The Prayer of the Little Ducks

Dear God,
give us a flood of water.
Let it rain tomorrow and always.
Give us plenty of little slugs
and other luscious things to eat.
Protect all folk who quack
and everyone who knows how to swim.
Amen.

*Carmen Bernos de Gasztold*
*translated by Rumer Godden*

# Lamplighter Barn

I can play
in the prickly hay
and I can find
where the chickens lay
and take off my shoes
and stay
and stay
in the tickly hay
on a rainy day.

*Myra Cohn Livingston*

# Slowly

Slowly the tide creeps up the sand,
Slowly the shadows cross the land.
Slowly the cart-horse pulls his mile,
Slowly the old man mounts the stile.

Slowly the hands move round the clock,
Slowly the dew dries on the dock.
Slow is the snail—but slowest of all
The green moss spreads on the old brick wall.

*James Reeves*

# Elsie Marley

Elsie Marley is grown so fine,
She won't get up to feed the swine,
But lies in bed till eight or nine.
Lazy Elsie Marley.

*Anon.*

# The Fairy Sleep and Little Bo-Peep

Little Bo-Peep,
Had lost her sheep,
And didn't know where to find them,
All tired she sank
On a grassy bank,
And left the birds to mind them.

Then the fairy, Sleep,
Took little Bo-Peep,
In a spell of dreams he bound her,
And silently brought
The flock she sought,
Like summer clouds around her.

When little Bo-Peep—
In her slumber deep—
Saw lambs and sheep together,
  All fleecy and white,
  And soft and light,
As clouds in July weather;

  Then little Bo-Peep
  Awoke from her sleep,
And laughed with glee to find them
  Coming home once more,
  The old sheep before,
And the little lambs behind them.

*Anon.*

27

# Mud

Take a bucket of soil.
Some water from a can.
Mix them well
in an old saucepan.
Add a few leaves.
Some flowerpetals too.
And soon you'll have
A Mudpie stew.

Take slugs and snails,
a scattering of sand.
Rub them round
with your muddy hand.
Leave in the sun
a while to bake.
And soon you'll have
A Mudpie cake.

*Ann Bonner*

# Little Brown Seed

Little brown seed, round and sound,
Here I put you in the ground.

You can sleep a week or two,
Then—I'll tell you what to do:

You must grow some downward roots,
Then some tiny upward shoots.

From those green shoots' folded sheaves
Soon must come some healthy leaves.

When the leaves have time to grow,
Next a bunch of buds must show.

Last of all, the buds must spread
Into blossoms white or red.

There, Seed! I've done my best.
Please to grow and do the rest.

*Rodney Bennett*

# Hickety, Pickety, my Black Hen

Hickety, pickety, my black hen,
She lays eggs for gentlemen;
Gentlemen come every day,
To see what my black hen doth lay.
Some days five and some days ten,
She lays eggs for gentlemen.

*Anon.*

# I had a Little Hen

I had a little hen,
The prettiest ever seen,
She washed me the dishes
And kept the house clean.

She went to the mill
To fetch me some flour,
She brought it home
In less than an hour.

She baked me my bread,
She brewed me my ale,
She sat by the fire
And told many a fine tale.

*Anon.*